THE ANAYA **SUN SIGN** *COMPANIONS*

AQUARIUS

20 January-19 February

CELESTINE O'RYAN

ANAYA PUBLISHERS LIMITED
LONDON

First published in Great Britain in 1991 by
Anaya Publishers Ltd., Strode House, 44-50 Osnaburgh Street, London NW1 3ND

ASTROLOGICAL CONSULTANT Jan Kurrels

Managing Editor	Judy Martin
Art Director	Nigel Osborne
Designers	Sally Stockwell
	Anne Clue
Illustrators	Marion Appleton
	David Ashby
	Lorraine Harrison
	Tony Masero
Indexer	Peter Barber

British Library Cataloguing in Publication Data
O'Ryan, Celestine
Aquarius. – (Anaya sun sign companions).
1. Astrology
I. Title
133.52
ISBN 1-85470-100-2

TYPESET IN GREAT BRITAIN BY MIDFORD TYPESETTING LTD, LONDON
COLOUR ORIGINATION IN SINGAPORE BY COLUMBIA OFFSET LTD
PRINTED IN SINGAPORE BY TIMES OFFSET LTD

CONTENTS

INTRODUCTION 6

THE ZODIAC 8

ZODIACAL INFLUENCES 10

THE AQUARIUS PERSONALITY 12

THE PLANETARY RULER 14

PATTERNS IN THE STARS 16

THE ATTRACTION OF OPPOSITES 18

THE SYMBOLS OF THE ZODIAC 20

THE HOUSE OF AQUARIUS 22

ELEMENTS AND QUALITIES 24

THE ZODIAC GARDEN 26

ASTROLOGY AND THE ARK 28

AQUARIUS ON THE MAP 30

EARTH'S BOUNTY 32

A HEAVENLY HERBAL 34

THE CELESTIAL BODY 36

THE STARS AND THE STONES 38

ZODIAC TREASURE 40

EARTH'S HIDDEN POWER 42

AQUARIUS ON THE CARDS 44

INDEX 46

20 JANUARY - 19 FEBRUARY

AQUARIUS

Most people know their own sun sign, and you know that yours is Aquarius, but do you appreciate its full impact on every area of your life? Your Sun Sign Companion *is a guide to the many pleasures and preferences that are specific to you as an Aquarian subject.*

Your personality profile is here – and much more. You can find out not only where you fit into the grand astrological scheme and the ways the other zodiac signs connect with your own, but also discover the delights of the Aquarian foods that are your special delicacies; the plants that you should grow in your garden to enhance your Aquarian moods; the animals that you appreciate for their affinities to your sign and the pets that you as an Aquarian can easily love and live with; the ways in which you need to take care of your body, and how your health and well-being may be affected by the fact that you were born under Aquarius.

The fascinating range of this Sun Sign Companion *explains your temperament, your actions and the ways you live your life in zodiacal terms. You are independent and imaginative and your special element – Aquarian air – makes you perceptive and communicative; your planetary ruler Uranus, emperor of the heavens, promotes confidence in your own ideas. You have singular connections with the powers of the Earth itself – its gemstones, metals and crystals. And your zodiacal profile is underlined by your Aquarian connections to the ancient and mysterious arts of the Runes and the Tarot.*

This book provides you with the intriguing mosaic of influences, interests and attributes that build into the total picture of yourself as an Aquarian. More than any other zodiacal guide, your Sun Sign Companion *reveals to you the inherent fun and enjoyment of life under Aquarius.*

A Q U A R I U S

THE ZODIAC

When the ancient astrologers studied the sky at night, they tracked the obvious motion and changing shape of the Moon, but noted two other phenomena: the frosty grandeur of the fixed stars and the different movements of the five observable planets. Mercury, Venus, Mars, Jupiter and Saturn moved and weaved about the night sky in repeating patterns, always within the same narrow strip of the heavens. And in the day time, the Sun could be seen progressing along the centre of this strip on its apparent orbit. Most of the action, celestially speaking, appeared to take place in a restricted heavenly corridor. Astronomers and astrologers therefore gave priority to this ribbon of sky, and noted what else appeared in it.

Sharing the strip were twelve fixed star constellations, known from ancient times. They were Aries the Ram, Taurus the Bull, Gemini the Twins, Cancer the Crab, Leo the Lion, Virgo the Virgin, Libra the Balance, Scorpius the Scorpion, Sagittarius the Archer, Capricornus the Goat, Aquarius the Water Carrier and Pisces the Fishes. As most of the constellations are named after sentient creatures, the Greeks called this band of sky the zodiac, from their word meaning images of animals or living beings.

In astronomical terms, the constellations take up varying amounts of sky and exhibit different degrees of brightness. Astrologically, they are assigned equal prominence and importance, and are given equal 30-degree arcs of the celestial band. These are the signs of the zodiac, and the starting point on the celestial circle is 0 degrees Aries, which was the point of the vernal equinox over 4000 years ago when the zodiac was established.

The celestial jostling along the zodiacal corridor is explained by the fact that the planets orbit the Sun roughly in the same plane. Imagine yourself at the centre of a race track, timing a group of runners as they lap the circuit, each one running at a different pace and in a different lane. Soon you would be able to predict when each one would pass you, especially if you noted down landmarks along the spectator stands behind the runners.

In the same way, astrologers pinpoint the position and motion of any planet, using the zodiac band as a reference grid. Interpretation of the effects of planetary power filtered through the zodiac grid is the enduring fascination of astrology. The planets are extremely powerful, as signified by their having been awarded the names and attributes of the gods.

A Q U A R I U S

ZODIACAL INFLUENCES

Your sun sign is the zodiac sign that the Sun, the most powerful of the heavenly bodies, appears to be passing through from our viewpoint on Earth at the time of your birth. It takes the Sun one year to progress through all the signs, and it is the Sun's huge power, filtered through each sign in turn, that etches the broad character templates of the signs. Over the centuries, each sign has acquired its own repertory of characteristics and personality traits, a seamless blend of archetypal myth and particular observation. So now we can talk about, say, a 'typical Aquarius' with the expectation that others will know what we mean. However, fine tuning and modification of the individual personality are dictated by two conditions at the time of birth – the positions of the Moon and planets in the zodiac and the nature of the ascendant, the sign rising on the eastern horizon at the moment of birth.

The Earth spins counter-clockwise daily on its axis, but to us it appears that the Sun, stars and planets wheel overhead from east to west. Within this framework, the zodiac passing overhead carries with it one sign every two hours; therefore the degree of the ascendant changes likewise, which explains why two people born on the same day can have such varying personalities. The influence of the ascending sign, and any planet positioned in it, has a strong bearing on the formation of the personality. An Aquarian with Pisces in the ascendant is quite a different kettle of fish to one with Gemini ascending.

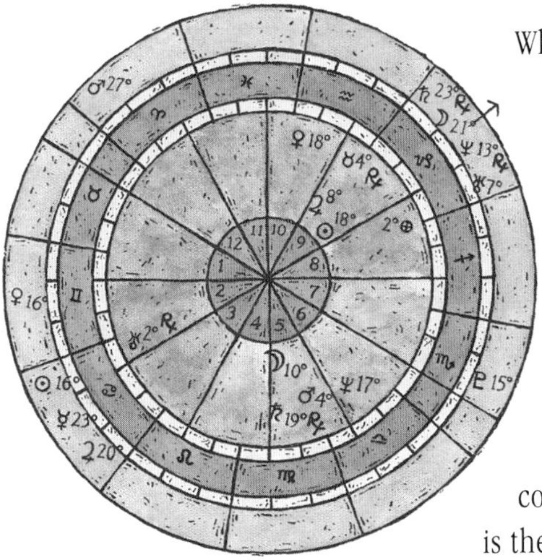

When an astrologer prepares a birth chart, or horoscope, for an individual, it is a two-dimensional record of these three-dimensional events in the heavens, represented graphically as a wheel encompassing concentric rings. The Earth is the pinpoint at the centre of the wheel and is surrounded by twelve fixed segments representing the zodiacal Houses, the areas of life in which planetary influences will manifest themselves. The outer circle of the chart represents the moving zodiacal corridor, divided into its twelve segments – the signs of the zodiac.

The predictability of the planets' movements has enabled astrologers to create tables, known as Ephemerides, of the planetary positions past, present and future. Once the positions of the Sun, Moon and planets have been established for a specific time, and a particular subject, the astrologer can assess and interpret what effects the planets will have, how they will enhance, diminish or frustrate each other's powers, and which areas of the subject's life will come under their particular influences. And all of this information is blended with the astrologer's understanding of the sun sign personality, the broad framework of individuality in zodiacal terms.

A Q U A R I U S

THE AQUARIUS PERSONALITY

Aquarius is the eleventh sign of the zodiac. Humane, idealistic, altruistic, Aquarius is the champion of the underdog; Aquarians abhor social injustices and inequalities, and will put themselves on the line to achieve social reform or lead the revolution against repression. Liberty, fraternity and equality are self-evident life rules to Aquarius.

In spite of this deep concern for humanity, Aquarians appear curiously remote and coolly aloof to the rest of the zodiac signs, who find it difficult to get close to them. Aquarians need lots of space, of the social and personal as well as the physical kind, but they are, paradoxically, very social beings. However, they may find close family ties oppressive, and prefer to put their energies into clubs, societies and movements, where people meet willingly out of mutual interests and concerns.

Individual, unpredictable and intuitive, Aquarians are very sure of their own minds, and do not care a fig if they appear eccentric or *outré* to the rest of the world. Their lightning perception and swift, analytical minds usually put them several steps ahead of the field, and their imaginative, extrapolative ideas are often light years ahead of their time. Here is the 'mad professor' of the zodiac, an indefatigable seeker of truth and knowledge who is unafraid to follow an idea or a concept wherever it leads. Yet Aquarians are full of optimism for the future of the human race; they mean science and technology to be the salvation of humanity, not the means of its destruction.

Aquarius
Orbis Regens
Uranus
Signum Obstans
Leo

AQUARIUS

THE PLANETARY RULER

Ancient astrologers named the five planets they could see in the night sky after the five most powerful classical gods; naturally, the planets took on the attributes and associations of the gods, and a pleasingly symmetrical system was devised to distribute this planetary power throughout the zodiac.

The Sun and Moon, being the most dazzling lights, ruled one sun sign each (Leo and Cancer). The remaining ten signs managed under the shared patronage of the five planets. Mercury presided over Gemini and Virgo, Venus over Taurus and Libra, Mars over Aries and Scorpio, Jupiter over Sagittarius and Pisces, and Saturn over Aquarius and Capricorn.

When more planets were discovered after the invention of the telescope in 1610, a reshuffle became necessary. Uranus (discovered in 1781) was allocated to Aquarius, Neptune (1836) was thought appropriate for Pisces, and Pluto (1930) now broods over Scorpio. This has unbalanced the symmetry: the search is on for other planets to share the burden with Venus and Mercury. Indeed, the asteroid Chiron, discovered in 1977 looping the void

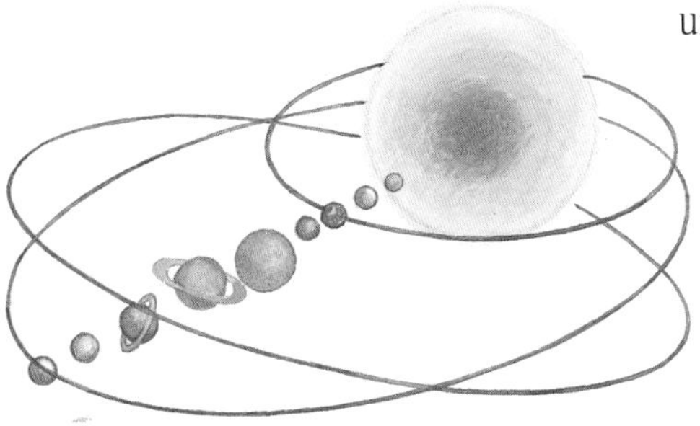

between Saturn and Uranus, is considered by some astrologers to be the suitable governor of Virgo.

The planetary power behind Aquarius now comes from Uranus, emperor of the heavens. Originally, Aquarius was assigned to Saturn, but this cautious, conventional, disciplined planet never

did seem to entirely explain the intuitive, offbeat, idealistic Aquarian persona, although Saturnine aloofness and emotional reserve are certainly strong Aquarian traits. Uranus represents original thinking, inventiveness, humanitarianism, and an abhorrence of restriction of any kind; it is also strongly associated with science and the technology of communication. It promotes practical kindness and confidence in one's own ideas. Adversely it can encourage unamiable eccentricity, crankiness, perversity and a wooden-headed conviction in the rightness of one's own opinion.

Astronomically, Uranus is the seventh planet from the Sun in the solar system, the first to be discovered by telescope. It is more than four times the size of Earth, with a ring system and fifteen known moons. Its axis is tilted to 98 degrees, lying almost in the same plane as its orbit, so that the poles are presented towards the Sun and Earth. Uranus takes 84 years to orbit the Sun.

In classical mythology, Uranus was one of the first gods, an ancient, savage god of the heavens. Son and consort of the all-powerful earth goddess Ge, he fathered a fearsome brood: the Centimani, or hundred-handed giants, the Cyclopes and the Titans. Uranus was deposed by one of these sons, the Titan Cronos (Saturn), who unmanned his father with a flint sickle.

A Q U A R I U S

PATTERNS IN THE STARS

Star pictures, or images of the constellations, are formed in the eye of the beholder. What we see as a neighbourly cluster is usually an optical illusion, the stars in the group being many light years apart. Even so, the urge to impose a friendly pattern on the frosty immensity of the night sky, to link the stars with the myths and legends on Earth, has been irresistible to all cultures. Different cultures make out different pictures, and the results are sometimes inscrutable – searching for Leo, say, you will look in vain for the shape of a lion pricked out in stars against the dark backcloth of the night sky.

The zodiac constellations were among the first to be made out, as they were the star groups that formed the background to the moving planets, providing a useful reference grid to plot planetary movements. These gave their names to the signs of the zodiac, although they spread unevenly across the sky and are not tidily

confined to the equal 30-degree segments of the imaginary zodiac band. Most stars are known by their Arabic names, and the star that shone brightest in each constellation when Arabic astrologers first compiled their star catalogues was designated its alpha.

The constellation that gave its name to the eleventh sign of the zodiac is Aquarius the Water Carrier, a southern star group tucked under the celestial equator. Aquarius is the second largest zodiacal constellation after Virgo, but is curiously indefinable, having no fixed pattern apart from the three stars forming a Y-shaped figuration that represents the Water Carrier's jar. There are fewer spectacular stars than you would expect from a constellation of such breadth: currently the brightest star is the beta, Sadalsuud, but the alpha is Aquarii Sadalmelik. Aquarius is home to the brightest planetary nebula in the sky, the Helix Nebula, as well as the Saturn Nebula, two globular clusters and several galaxies.

If the constellation is enigmatic, the myth behind it is equally difficult to establish. The Egyptians associated it with the Hapi, the powerful water god whose two jars were the source of the mighty Nile. From further back in time comes the Sumerian-Babylonian myth of Ea, the fish-antelope, who emerged from his submarine palace to teach humanity the facts of moral life. More usually associated with Capricorn, Ea was also known as 'the god of streams' and has an oblique connection with the water god of sources. According to certain Greek myths, however, Aquarius is the starry image of Ganymede, the devastatingly beautiful youth chosen by the gods of Olympus as their cup-bearer. Zeus became so besotted by Ganymede's beauty that he made him immortal and placed him among the stars to pour out nectar and ambrosia forever.

THE ATTRACTION OF OPPOSITES

In astrological terms, polarity describes the strong complementary relationship between signs that are exactly opposite each other on the zodiac circle, 180 degrees or six signs apart. These signs share the same gender – masculine or feminine – and the same quality – cardinal, fixed or mutable – and so share the ways they look at the world and shape their energy. Characteristics and interests complement each other or harmonize on different scales.

Relationships between polar signs are often very satisfying and fruitful, especially in the context of work. A clue to this affinity lies with the elements governed by each sign. The mathematics of polarity mean that earth signs oppose only water signs, and that fire opposes only air. Fire and air signs therefore encourage and inspire each other – fire cannot burn without air and air needs heat to rise. Earth and water signs conspire together creatively – earth without water is unfruitful, water unconfined by earth wastes its energy in diffusion – and together they make mud, rich material for any creative process.

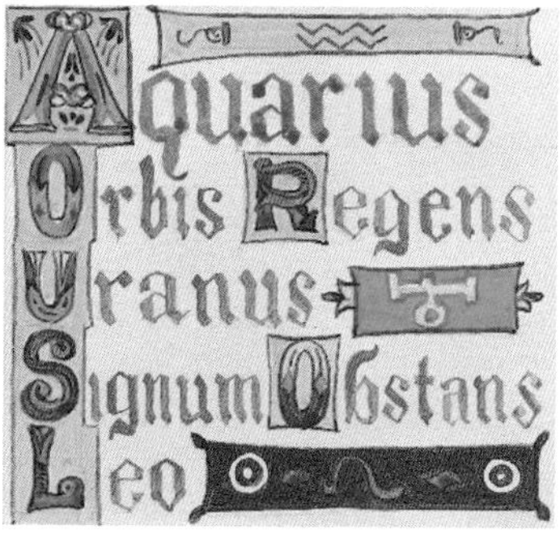

Six signs away from independent, unconventional Aquarius, the eccentric observer who sees life as a spectator sport, preferring the view from the edge, we find sociable, generous, limelight-loving Leo, the life and soul of the party who cannot bear to be anywhere but the centre of the circle. Warm-hearted, magnanimous Leo, who takes the direct approach to every relationship in life, personal or professional, must seem absurdly over-committed to cool, aloof Aquarius, who takes a detached scientific interest in fellow humans, analysing their behaviour and drawing some ironic conclusions. Below the surface, however, a shared and complementary shaping energy is at work, the fixed energy of consolidation.

Both Aquarius and Leo preside over pivotal times of the year, when the seasonal die has been cast and the Earth is held in temporary balance. Everything is fixed in a time of consolidated growth before harvest, or in the final hours before the earth's winter repose is broken by the vigorous sprouting of new growth. Aquarius, the air sign, embraces universality, diffusing ideas to reach as many people as possible; Leo, the fire sign, burns as a beacon, a focus for society.

The complementary aspect of polarity is also seen in the characteristics traditionally associated with the two signs. Both are concerned with the good ordering of humanity, Aquarius by setting out political and sociological theories and structures that will enable people to govern themselves, while Leo leads by example and charisma.

A Q U A R I U S

THE SYMBOLS OF THE ZODIAC

Ever since astrology began, there has been a kind of astrological shorthand, a set of symbols or ideograms called glyphs. Glyphs make the language of astrology universal and available to people who have no literary tradition. They also make it a lot easier to draw up a birth chart, being a convenient form of notation, especially where planets are clustered in one area of the chart.

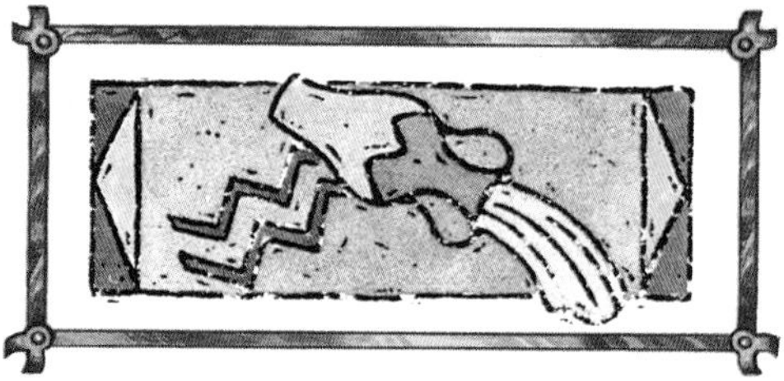

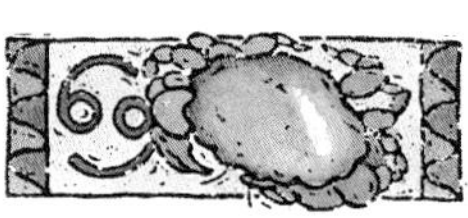

Each of the zodiac signs has its own glyph, as do the planets. They have evolved over centuries, and so are now freighted with symbolism, not simply convenient codes.

Today, the glyph for Aquarius is a deceptively simple, austere graphic, two parallel zigzag lines. This economically elegant symbol has remained much the same throughout its astrological history. Early Egyptians used a hieroglyph of three similar lines. The Greeks used two symbols,

one a simple pattern of three short, straight parallel lines, the other an indeterminate, rather elongated and wavery Z-shape. Medieval astrologers had two versions, one a small row of joined hoops mirrored by an inverted row of hoops underneath it, the other a prototype of the modern glyph.

There is a special fascination in studying the glyphs to see what other symbolism may be contained within them. In one simple, economical pattern the Aquarius glyph indicates at once the ripple of water and the unimpeded flow of electrical energy through the air, the free flow of knowledge – it is not water Aquarius pours from his urn, but liquid from the well of human truth and knowledge. The zigzags and oscillations indicate compacted power and the double lines signal abundance. Here is harnessed energy, knowledge and power used for human good.

The planets also have their glyphs, and the Uranus symbol is a circle surmounted by a short perpendicular line, superimposed by an H; the whole effect irresistibly brings to mind the antenna of a communications aerial.

A Q U A R I U S

THE HOUSE OF AQUARIUS

The twelve Houses are an intellectual concept, not a physical reality, an expression of all the aspects of human life and experience, from the self to the infinite. Each is associated with a sign of the zodiac, sharing its planetary ruler and elemental energy. However, the Houses are fixed and constant – they are represented by the central numbered segments on a birth chart – and the signs and planets pass through them. They are the channels through which planetary and zodiacal energies flow and indicate which area of life is the focus of particular zodiacal influence at any one time.

Aquarius, being the eleventh sign of the zodiac, is associated with the Eleventh House, which is also overseen by Aquarius's planetary ruler, Uranus. Like Aquarius, it is permeated with air energy, and therefore concerns itself with mental and intellectual activity, all levels of communication and social interaction. In particular, the Eleventh House is concerned with intellectual pleasures and recreations, clubs and societies, friends and acquaintances brought together by mutual interests, and the wider pattern of social life. The Eleventh House is an easy, friendly place, the meeting

place for an informal society of like-minded people, to share the brotherhood and sisterhood of humanity unencumbered by emotional ties.

When Uranus is in the Eleventh House in a birth chart, it stimulates the subject's aims and ideals in life and intensifies the Aquarian enthusiasm for becoming involved with social groups or scientific projects (Uranus is also specially associated with astronomy and astrology). It encourages a talent for intuitive, unemotional friendships.

ELEMENTS AND QUALITIES

It was Aristotle, the great Greek thinker, who formalized the idea that all life is made up from infinitely various permutations of the four elements – fire, earth, air and water. In the zodiac cycle there are three signs representing each element. Aries, Leo and Sagittarius are for fire; Taurus, Virgo and Capricorn for earth; Gemini, Libra and Aquarius for air; and Cancer, Scorpio and Pisces for water. However, in each case, the element is filtered through a different kind, or quality, of energy field; cardinal, fixed and mutable (or transforming). Aries, Cancer, Libra and Capricorn are cardinal; Taurus, Leo, Scorpio and Aquarius are fixed; Gemini, Virgo, Sagittarius and Pisces are mutable. Each sign is a unique manifestation of one element and one quality of energy.

Air is the Aquarian element: lucid and liberating, the breath of life, essential for a clear head, clear eye and clear mind, the prerequisites of unbiased judgement. Air is the natural element of the mental life, the home of ideas, perceptions, communication. Yet air is by no means powerless in the material world. This is the element that can gently fan your overheated brow or savagely rip the roof off your home, bring rainclouds to refresh parched crops or work itself up into a hurricane to devastate whole cities.

Aquarian air is the whole spacious arch of the heavens, the universal element shared by everybody, the element that we all breathe and that no one can annexe for their personal use. Aquarians need lots of space, personal and physical, and like to walk through the world with an invisible, distancing air cushion between them and their fellows. Many Aquarians are keenly interested in flying and, like Leonardo da Vinci, may dream of silent, self-propelled human flight.

Aquarian energy is fixed. Fixed energy people are the consolidators, the builders, the steadfast guardians of their particular energy. Uranus, Aquarius's ruler, is the great sky god, lord of the boundless skies, who grants Aquarians the space to pursue truth and knowledge to their minds' content.

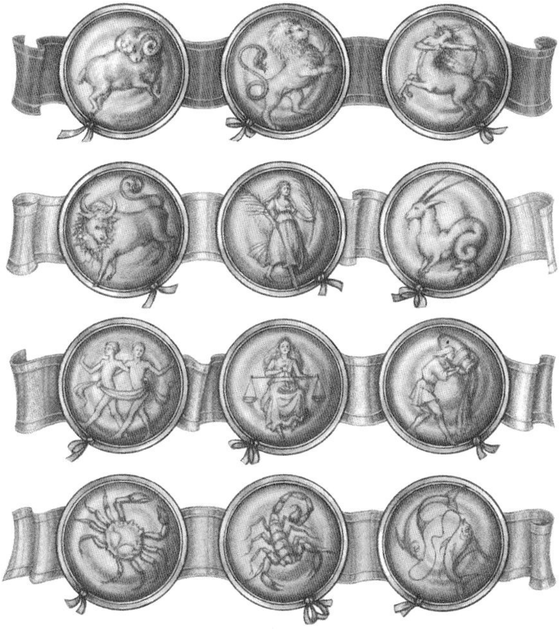

A Q U A R I U S

THE ZODIAC GARDEN

Aquarius bowling through the country lanes in an eccentric vintage roadster or state-of-the-art personal transporter likes to see food growing, to see agricultural technology at work – huge, immensely complicated harvesters that dig sugar beet out of the earth at one end and more or less dispense bags of refined sugar at the other – or people working the land in teams, cooperating towards the common good. Best of all, Aquarians would like to be piloting a private plane, winging over endless orchards full of fruit trees.

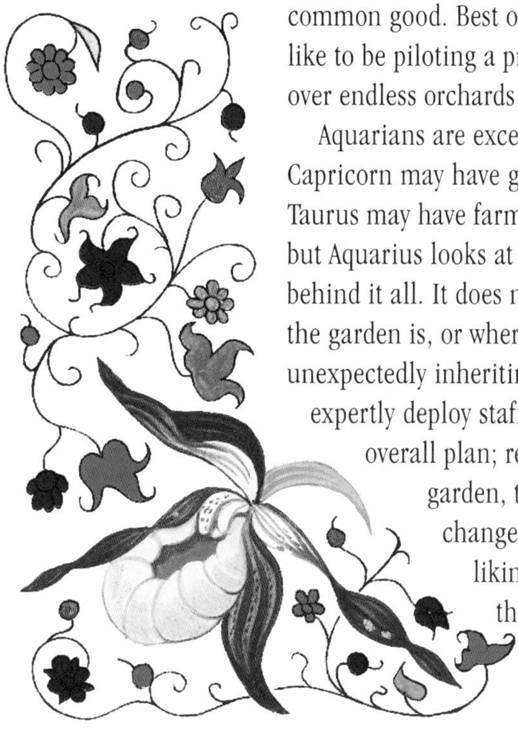

Aquarians are excellent gardeners; Capricorn may have green fingers and Taurus may have farming bred in the bone, but Aquarius looks at the scientific method behind it all. It does not matter what size the garden is, or where it is: Aquarians unexpectedly inheriting a vast estate will expertly deploy staff to carry out their overall plan; restricted to a suburban garden, they will happily change the horizons to their liking; confined to a patio, they will conjure horticultural miracles from containers.

In the ideal Aquarian garden, fruit and vegetables come first, perhaps because they lend themselves to experiment: breeding back to old-fashioned flavoursome apples, for example, or breeding forward for better cropping varieties of pears. Expect to see fruit trees, peaches espaliered against a rosy old brick wall, melons, asparagus beds, celery trenches, climbing French beans, unusual kinds of potato, tomatoes and grapes under glass or in the hothouse. Aquarians are attracted to the unusual – medlars, quinces and loquats, all relatives of the rose and the apple. They are also intrigued by vegetable extremes, and will try growing the world's heaviest onion or portliest leek, not for competitive reasons but purely in the interests of science.

Aquarian flowers are fresh, simple, and often yellow: daffodils, primroses, daisies, old-fashioned yellow roses. Aquarius also flirts with the gorgeous (though poisonous) cascades of bright, butter-coloured laburnum, the golden rain tree. In the house, elegant cut flowers are usually preferred over pot plants; but the secret sybarite that dwells in the souls of most Water Carriers surrenders totally to the exotic beauty of orchids.

A Q U A R I U S

ASTROLOGY AND THE ARK

The word zodiac comes from the Greek word for living creatures, and many of the signs are symbolized by animals. Aquarius, however, is among the minority represented by human figures. In this case, the image is a mature man generously pouring out an endless supply of liquid from the well of knowledge, pooling the human resource to the benefit of all.

On the face of it, Aquarius has no direct and obvious connection with animals. Individualistic Aquarius is possibly too independent to need or want pets. Aquarians' strong humanitarian instinct may lead them to throw their energies (and money) into supporting societies and organizations that help or care for animals in general rather than focus on individuals. A single eccentric cat or an independent-minded dog may thrive in an Aquarian household, but there will be nothing in a cage. Some Aquarians like to emphasize their eccentric streak with offbeat pets – a non-barking basenji hound perhaps, a Manx cat, or a free-living mynah bird who quotes Einstein.

Yet there are animals traditionally assigned to Aquarius: these are the large birds capable of hours of uninterrupted long-haul flying – condors and eagles, albatrosses and herring gulls, the lords of the air, the Aquarian element. Effortlessly riding the thermals high above the messy scrum of human activity, they cast down an ironic glance, taking a wide, bird's-eye view of the frantic doings of society, able to scan horizons that those toiling below do not even know exist. Independent, strong, self-sufficient, bound to no personal place, the great birds of the air are the quintessential symbol of freedom.

A Q U A R I U S

AQUARIUS ON THE MAP

Mundane astrology charts the birth of nations: countries, cities and major towns come under zodiacal influence, just as their inhabitants do. Often the ascendant, the sign in the First House which characterizes the nation as a whole, is more significant than the sun sign. Various methods are used to assess which zodiac sign holds sway where. Countries with an incontestable birthday – 4 July 1776 for the USA, for instance – have a standard birth chart. In countries which have evolved more organically, zodiacal influences may be deduced by the broad characteristics – can you think of a more suitable ruling sign than Taurus for Switzerland, the land loud with cowbells? Cities and towns may show their zodiacal allegiance by their function – most spas are ruled by health-conscious Virgo, and many ports are ruled by Cancer, the home-loving sailor of the zodiac.

Aquarius's worldly subjects include Sweden, Israel and the USSR. Sweden is the embodiment of the Aquarian humane ideal: a cool spacious country with a superlative social welfare system, dedicated to safety and provision for all its inhabitants. And it is the birthplace of Alfred Nobel (1833-96), who accidentally invented dynamite, made a fortune from it, and left most of the money to provide prizes for the world's finest scientists, writers and peacemakers. Israel, re-established in 1948 after a lapse of over one-and-a-half millenia, owes its dazzling economic and social

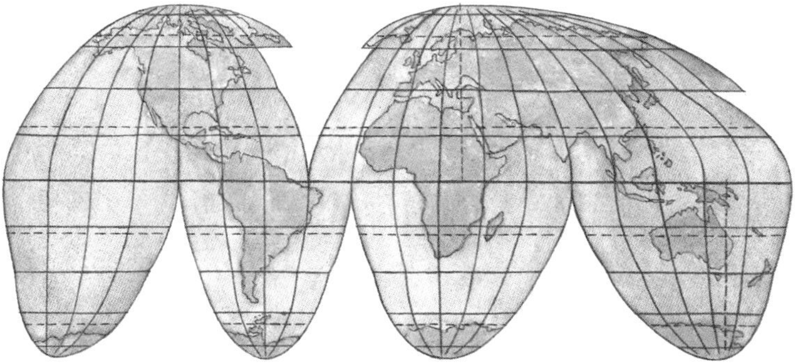

progress to its *kibbutzim*, the collective, cooperative farms and camps, where the altruistic (and very successful) rule is all for one and one for all. The USSR reflects the other, revolutionary side of Aquarius: the momentous events of October 1917 that overthrew Czarist Russia and established the soviet ideal were the template for revolution twentieth-century style; and today, on the brink of the age of Aquarius, the USSR is once again the scene of upheaval and dislocation.

Cities under Aquarius include Salzburg, birthplace and home of the sublime Mozart, himself an Aquarian; Leningrad, named for the father of the Russian revolution, Vladimir Ilyich Lenin; Moscow, Bremen and Hamburg.

A Q U A R I U S

EARTH'S BOUNTY

Astute Aquarius shares a harvest of food plants with Capricorn and Taurus. Their traditional ruler Saturn gives Aquarians legitimate claim to Capricorn's onions, potatoes, cabbage and barley; but they favour Taurean foods because they are simply the best – wheat and cereals, apples and pears, berry fruits and grapes. Put these together with a fondness for meat of all kinds, and you have the basic ingredients for a very rich menu indeed – which is rather a shame, as Aquarians should stick to a light diet for the sake of their hearts and blood pressure. Sometimes they find this very difficult and are prone to binge eating and crash dieting.

Although Aquarius raids the larders of its zodiacal neighbours, Aquarians have a special preference of their own, for preserved food of all kinds, food that can be stored when it is abundant for everybody's benefit when times are hard: salt beef, pastrami, salami, ham and bacon, wind-dried sausages, smoked and cured meat; dried fruit, pickles, preserves, mincemeat, salted nuts, exotic fruits relaxing blissfully in unusual liqueurs. Aquarians are very partial to spices, once the only way to preserve perishable meat; and the invention of the deep freeze was deeply satisfying to the Aquarian mind.

Dining with Aquarius is a pleasant experience; Aquarius assembles the guest list with as much care as the menu, hand-picking suitable friends to guarantee an easygoing, stimulating evening. And the food will be good but unpredictable: you may get a pungent madras curry with all the trimmings one evening, the best sausage and mash you ever tasted the next, and an elaborate seafood supper with everything from cockles to lobster on the third. But there will always be fruit – interesting varieties of apples and pears, or unusual fruit such as pomegranates, medlars, quinces. Expect good white wine from unusual vineyards, champagne if Aquarius is feeling flush, and delicious specialist liqueurs and spirits.

Aquarius enjoys dining out, but with like-minded friends, not the madding crowd. Aquarians may well join a wine or food society or dining club to combine good company with good food. No foodie snob, unpredictable Aquarius dines all over the culinary map: a truckers' diner for magnificent breakfasts; speciality ethnic restaurants for Pekin duck, *linghuini*, or chicken soup with *kneidlech*; a squillion-star chef's palace for a gourmet blow-out; or a burger bar for steak and fries.

AQUARIUS

A HEAVENLY HERBAL

Herbs and the heavens have been linked forever; for many centuries, herbs were the only medicine, and the gathering and application of them were guided by the planets. Doctors would learn the rudiments of astrology as a matter of course – Hippocrates claimed that 'a physician without a knowledge of astrology had no right to call himself a physician'.

Healing plants and their ruling planets were often linked via the elements – fire, water, air and earth. Mars, for example, a hot fiery planet, self-evidently rules over hot, fiery plants such as mustard. Herbs that cure the ills of particular parts of the body are ruled by the planet that governs that part of the body. Plants are also assigned according to what they look like. For example, walnuts, which look like tiny models of the brain, are ruled by Mercury, the planet which rules the brain.

All herbs are more effective if they are gathered on a day ruled by their patron planet, especially at dawn, when they are fat with sap drawn up by the beams of the Moon, or at dusk, after a day basking in the strengthening rays of the Sun.

After an independent survey of the herbal catalogue, Aquarius takes cuttings from the herb gardens of the zodiac's two top gardeners, Taurus and Capricorn, selecting the offbeat, unusual strong tasting or spicy specimens. Hemp and hemlock, both extremely poisonous but capable of healing in the right hands, come via Capricorn, ruled by Saturn, Aquarius's traditional ruler,

Hemp is powerful against intestinal troubles; roast hemlock is reputedly good for gout (Aquarius loves good things, and can overdose on good red wine and bloody meat) but it must never be used by the untrained herbalist, as it is extremely poisonous – hemlock tea was the ancient Greek instrument of state execution. Unfortunately, hemlock looks very much like its blameless cousin, parsley, of which Aquarius is very fond, so gathering of wild parsley stalks is to be avoided.

From the well-stocked Taurean garden comes heartsease, or pansy, the cultivated violet, an old folk remedy for infant convulsions. Favourite culinary herbs for Water Carriers are the bitter-leaved sorrel, pungent cloves (to bring out the best in apples) and, especially, blood-cleansing mint in all its varieties – peppermint, spearmint, apple mint and watermint. Aquarius also shares Taurus's fondness for spices of all kinds, the hotter and more unusual the better.

AQUARIUS

THE CELESTIAL BODY

Each part of the body comes under the influence of a different zodiac sign. Aquarius rules the shins, the ankles and the circulation of the blood. Aquarians of both sexes are justifiably vain about their well-turned ankles, but are more than usually likely to suffer from sprains, twists and breaks, not to mention bruised and battered shins. Varicose veins and hardening of the arteries may also plague Aquarians in later life.

As the part of the body ruled by the polar sign is important in health matters, so Aquarians should take care of heart, back and spine, ruled by Leo. A light diet, regular exercise, and resisting the urge to take life to the limit will help preserve Aquarian health.

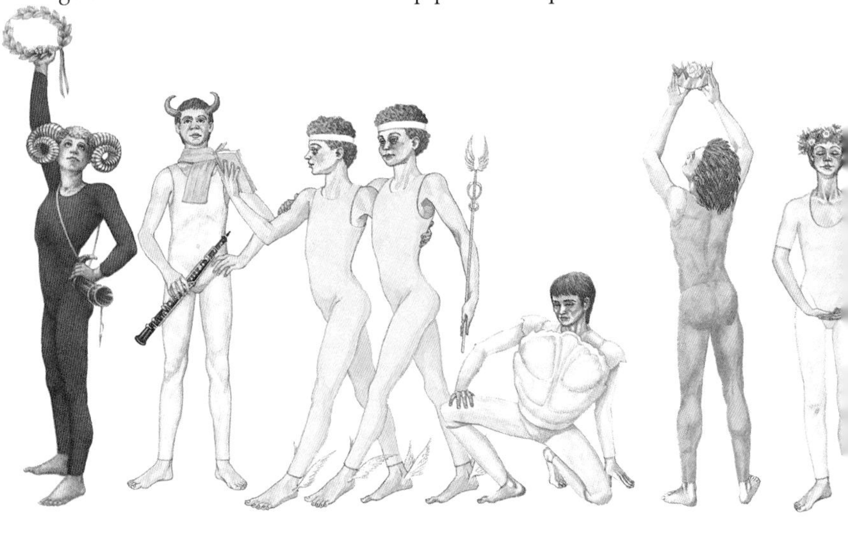

Uranus, Aquarius's ruling planet, looks after the whole circulatory system and the mysterious pineal body in the centre of the brain, the so-called 'third eye', whose function is unknown. French philosopher René Descartes considered it the home of the soul.

Keeping themselves warm and their circulation on the move should be the Aquarian health aim. Rather too individualistic for team games, Aquarians would do better to join a swimming club or a dance or fitness class to keep in shape. If they are unwell, they may turn to holistic medicine, especially acupuncture which is based on unblocking or stimulating the flow of *chi*, the life force, around the body.

After a hard day casting a benign eye over the world, Aquarius can relax and dream in a bath laced with warming oils to stimulate the circulation – ginger, black pepper, cinnamon, juniper berry, rosemary.

A Q U A R I U S

THE STARS AND THE STONES

Runes are a code, secret keys to the different facets of the whole interconnecting universe. Originated by the Germanic nomads who wandered the plains of northern Italy some 500 years before Christ, this compact and portable form of magic crossed the Alps and spread throughout northern Europe and Scandinavia. The twenty-four 'letters' of the *futharc* (an acronym of the first six letters of the runic alphabet) were used by the pragmatic Germans as a straightforward recording medium, as well as a shortcut to tapping the secrets of the universe. Each rune is a powerpacked symbol of one aspect of existence – for example, the fourth rune *As* means ash tree, but also signifies the tree of the world, the divine force that controls the cosmic order.

When the runes are cast, they combine, and the trained runemaster can read what has been, what is, and what influences are shaping future events. Authentic ancient runes, the portable arkana, were carved or painted on fresh-cut fruitwood and cast onto a white cloth for divination, but pebble or stone runes work just as well. Everyone should make their own runes – they have personal power, and they are free.

Runic astrology divides the sky into twenty-four segments, or seles, which correspond with the futharc. The seles modify the expression of planetary energy as each planet passes through them. The planets carry the attributes of the northern gods, and these too have runic associations.

As the sun signs do not coincide with the runic seles, they often come under the influence of two or more runes. The Aquarius runes are *Peorth*, *Elhaz* and *Sigel*. *Peorth* has a general meaning

of social gathering for fun and enjoyment and the specific meaning of pawn or piece on a board game. We are all pawns in life's game, and *Peorth* signifies the individual urge to reconcile free will with fate, to lead a life as independent and self-determined as possible within the larger context of destiny. *Elhaz*, whose literal meaning is elk, the animal, or elk-sedge, a tough, resilient fenland plant, is the most important rune for Aquarius. A strong-minded defender and protector of the common good, *Elhaz* represents the triumph of rugged individualism, the enduring validity of idealism. *Sigel*, the Sun, is the daily triumph of light over darkness, a creative, uplifting rune that brings confidence in one's own ideas. The runic image of Aquarius – heroically individualistic, independent, idealistic and altruistic, excited by new ideas and confident in the progress and perfectability of humanity – is remarkably similar to the zodiacal profile.

Planetary rulers have their own runes. The northern equivalent of Aquarius's ruler Uranus is Urd, the first of the three Norns, or Fates, who personifies disruptive change, revolution and reformation, the unleashing of powers which may lead upward to enlightenment or downward to pointless, violent destruction. Urd's rune is *Ur*, the wild ox, meaning raw, undifferentiated, unshaped creative power.

A Q U A R I U S

ZODIAC TREASURE

The zodiac treasure hoard may overflow with gorgeous gems, but it is guarded by grumpy and confused dragons, who squabble among themselves and cannot agree on which stone best fits which sign. However, the beguiling idea of a jewelled girdle encircling the zodiac is an ancient one, and may even be based on the twelve gemstones, one for each of the tribes of Israel, set on the breastplate of the Jewish high priests of biblical times. Medieval astrologers felt reasonably sure of their ground and listed the gems as follows, in zodiacal order: bloodstone, sapphire, agate, emerald, onyx, carnelian, chrysolite, aquamarine, topaz, ruby, garnet and amethyst. Catherine de Medici, the original power-dresser, was rumoured to possess a glittering belt of zodiacal gems.

As there is no real consensus in the matter, a new approach is needed. Consideration of the colour and characteristics traditionally attributed to each sun sign may lead to a satisfying match of sign with stone.

Aquarian colours cluster round the blue band of the spectrum: the colours of the sky, from the pale rosy turquoise of dawn to the electric blue of dusk. Aquamarine is often cited as the Aquarian stone, but Aquarius can also choose from a chestful of gorgeous gems on the basis of colour alone – turquoise, blue topaz, lapis lazuli or dark blue sapphires, associated with Aquarius's ancient ruler, Saturn. Another powerful Saturnine gem, the garnet, is also recommended for Aquarius, in spite of its dark red colour; ancient healers considered that it cured 'fevers of the blood' and could predict impending disaster by losing its lustre. Water Carriers may also consider the unusual zircon, or jacinth, a stone that shines bright and flawless as a diamond, but is not so hard; the blue variety known as 'starlite' is particularly stunning.

Aquarian gems should be set in shimmering metals – silver (stimulates the circulation), platinum, or white gold (a distant gleam of polar sign Leo) – for Aquarius is the secret magpie of the zodiac. When the going gets tough, tough Aquarians go shopping – for baubles, bangles, beads and earrings. Male Aquarians are rather fond of earrings, and may wear a discreet single stud – they like to feel dashing, unconventional and a little piratical. When jewellery buying for Aquarius, stick to light, modern designs and go for quality rather than quantity.

A Q U A R I U S

EARTH'S HIDDEN POWER

Beneath the earth, in the realm of Pluto, lie the solidified energies, metals and crystals that hum with compacted potency. The Aquarian metal is uranium, discovered in 1789 and named after the new planet Uranus, sighted only eight years before. Used in the right way, uranium can be very useful to humanity, but in the wrong hands it spells devastation. It certainly cannot be used to decorate the home or ornament the person.

Aquarians are much better off with aluminium, a wonderfully beneficent metal: light, bright, abundant, untarnishable and universally useful. It is also a modern metal, discovered in the nineteenth century; charmingly, the very first aluminium artefact was a baby's rattle made in the 1850s for the infant son of Napoleon III, the patron of the world's first aluminium factory in Paris. Aquarius favours cool, uncluttered interiors, and appreciates the light elegance of aluminium furniture and the unusual

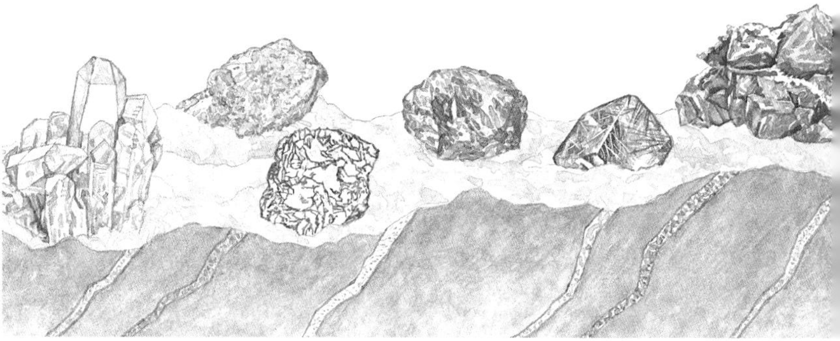

textures produced when this versatile metal is burnished to a high gloss or sandblasted to a dull matt finish.

Crystals are chemical elements compressed over millenia into dense, solid form, storehouses of electromagnetic energy. Most crystals associated with Aquarius can be worn as gemstones. Aquarius has a share in the huge crystalline power of the mighty protective amethyst, a powerful blood purifier and stimulator of the 'third eye', the transforming crystal that shatters illusions. Garnet (one of Aquarius's gemstones) supports and revitalizes the circulatory system.

Back-up crystals might include turquoise, which promotes loyal friendship and stimulates the circulation; lapis lazuli, blue topaz and blue tourmaline, all of which sharpen the sight of the 'third eye', and labradorite, the crystal expression of remoteness, physical and emotional. Aquarius can also use the crystalline power associated with its traditional ruler, Saturn: the tigereye, for independence of mind, and speckled turritella agate, the crystal of change. Uranus shares these stones, but also has botswana agate, the crystal that gleams with the exhilarating hint of the unexpected.

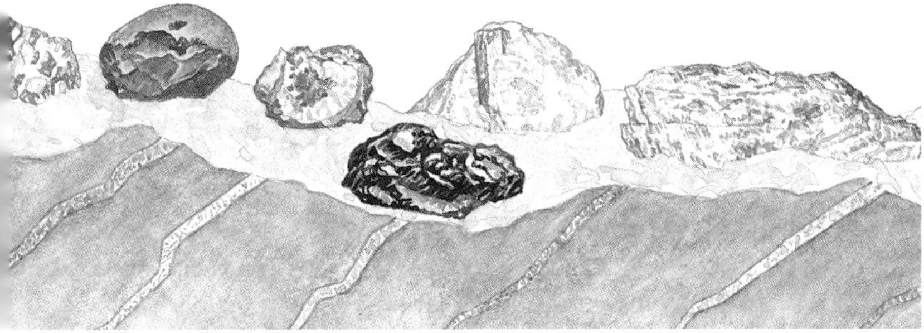

AQUARIUS ON THE CARDS

Sometimes called the Devil's Picture Book, the tarot was probably created in the twelfth century, but its origins are suitably shrouded in secrecy. There are seventy-eight cards: twenty-two in the Major Arcana, a gallery of enigmatic archetypal images from the Fool via the Wheel of Fortune to the World, and fifty-six in the Minor Arcana, divided into four suits – coins, cups, swords and batons (or wands).

Tarot cards, being one of the ways to explore the human psyche, have an affinity with the zodiac sun signs, and cards from the Major Arcana and the court cards from the Minor Arcana are associated with specific signs. If two cards are assigned, they should be considered together.

Traditionally, Aquarius is represented by one card, the Wheel of Fortune, the tenth card in the Major Arcana. An ancient concept that appears in some form in all cultures, the Wheel neatly symbolizes the essentially cyclic pattern of life and the cosmos, the change and flux of fortune, the transience of both glory and despair. None of us can get off the wheel, but an appreciation of its concept brings a liberating psychic wholeness, an ability to accept the constant change that marks the human condition and to weather fate's arbitrary blows. Adversely, the Wheel can signify someone lashed to life's treadmill, unable to learn from mistakes.

Aquarius's ruler Uranus is associated with the Tower, sometimes called *la Maison de Dieu*, the House of God. A proud brick-built tower, whose small, mean windows symbolize the restricted outlook of humanity, is devastated by a bolt of lightning from the heavens: the man-made construct destroyed by natural forces, illusion shattered by truth. The blasted tower means massive change and upheaval, the overthrow of old orders, the blowing away of artificial horizons, mould-breaking on a cosmic scale. Adversely, it can signify a mind imprisoned by its own narrow ideas and dogma, too inflexible to dodge the slings and arrows, a mind that brings avoidable destruction down upon itself.

There are many ways to lay out the tarot cards for a reading, but a particularly zodiacal one is to place the significator (the card chosen to represent the questioner) in the centre and lay out the other cards in a circle anticlockwise, starting from the are nine-o-clock position. This follows the layout of the astrological Houses, and the cards are interpreted in the context of the House in which they fall.

INDEX

air signs 18, 19, 22, 24-5
aluminium 42
animals 28-9
Aquarii Sadalmelik 17
Aristotle 24
ascendants 10

birds 29
body, the Aquarian 36-7
Bremen 31

Cancer 30
Capricorn 34
Catherine de Medici 40
Centimani 15
Chiron (asteroid) 14-15
cities 31
colours 40-1
constellations 8-9, 16-17
countries 30-1
Cronos 15
crystals 42, 43
Cyclopes 15

Ea 17
Earth 10, 19
earth signs 18, 24
elements, the four 24-5, 34
Ephemerides 11

farming 26
fire signs 18, 19, 24
flowers 26, 27, 35
food 27, 32-3, 36
fruits 27, 32, 33

Ganymede 17
gardens 26-7, 34-5
Ge 15
gemstones 40, 41, 43
glyphs 20-1

Hamburg 31
Hapi 17
health 32, 34-5, 36-7, 43
herbs 34-5, 37
Hippocrates 34
horoscopes 11

Israel 30-1

jewellery 40, 41
Jupiter 14

Leningrad 31
Leo 19, 41

Mars 14, 34
meats 32
Mercury 14, 34
metals 42-3
Moon 10, 11, 14, 34
Moscow 31

nebulae 17
Neptune 14
Nobel, Alfred 30

personality, the Aquarian
  12, 15, 18-19, 22-3,
  24-5
planets 8, 9, 10, 11,
  14-15, 21
plants 26-7, 32, 34-5
polarities 18-19
ports 30
runes 38-9

Sadalsuud 17
Salzburg 31
Saturn 14, 15, 34, 41,
spas 30
spices 32, 35
sports 37
stars 8-9, 16-17
Sun 8, 9, 10, 11, 14, 15,
Sweden 30
Switzerland 30

tarot 44-5
Taurus 30, 34, 35
Titans 15

uranium 42
Uranus 14, 15, 21, 22, 23
  25, 37, 39, 43, 45
Urd (Norn) 39
USSR 30, 31

vegetables 27, 32
Venus 14
Virgo 15, 30

water signs 18, 24

Zeus 17
zodiac:
  body 36-7
  elements 24
  Houses 22-3, 45
  influences 10-11
  origins 8-9, 14-15, 17
  symbols 20-1
  treasure 40-1